BEAUTY FREELY GIVEN : A UNIVERSAL TRUTH

BEAUTY FREELY GIVEN : A UNIVERSAL TRUTH

ARTEFACTS FROM THE COLLECTION OF ROBIN HANBURY-TENISON

Photographed & Arranged by Christopher John Bowden

Garage Press 2012

This book has been desighned and assembled by Christopher John Bowden at the Garage Press 2012

< Kalahari bushman's decorated ostrich egg

ISBN   978-0-9566803-3-4

GARAGE PRESS

Foreword

With his comprehensive understanding of ornamentation and man's desire to evolve form and decoration directly from nature, Owen Jones's theories, though conceived over a hundred and fifty years ago, show great insight into the basic truths of the world's varied cultural artistic intuitions. Jones rightly observes in his monumental *Grammar Of Ornament* (1856) that the works of "Savage Tribes" rank with the most sophisticated manufactures of the notable "developed nations", often excelling them.

The individual groups of objects reproduced within this catalogue, gifts given to Robin Hanbury-Tenison on his many travels, were made as gestures of friendship and simple generosity by pastoral peoples who were secure within their tenets of craftsmanship and organic design. Often the objects were precious to the giver, on occasions, the most treasured possessions of a most hospitable and Edenic existence.

It gives great satisfaction to see how a culture can evolve objects of use which are essentially mechanically sophisticated, but equally, completely successful as to form and decoration. In the nineteenth century, Pugin, Jones, Dresser and Morris all designed and manufactured with an individual understanding of utility and ornamentation which can give pleasure, even making the mundane beautiful. Whereas these nineteenth century masters of design often evolved their truth to the *spirit of form* through rigorous scholarship, the artefacts illustrated within this little volume were the creation of minds totally attuned to their environment, thus essentially a creation of the greater garden of our planet.

Graham Ovenden

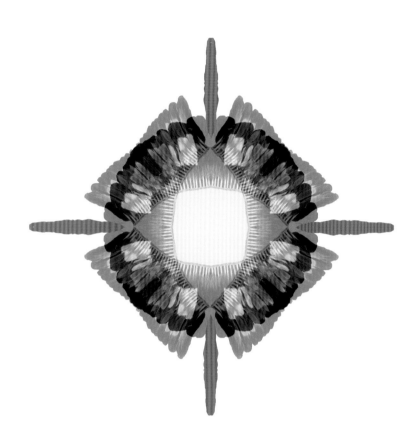

BEAUTY FREELY GIVEN

ARTEFACTS FROM THE COLLECTION OF ROBIN HANBURY-TENISON

These artefacts were mostly given to me by the people who made and wore or used them. I found the remote tribal people among whom I travelled in the fifties, sixties and seventies to be innately generous, so that they would insist on my accepting anything I admired. I would try to reciprocate with presents of my own, but that would often only result in even more beautiful objects being thrust upon me. These are mostly workaday goods, constructed for practical purposes but made with consummate skill so that they become artefacts of great beauty, even though they were usually expected to be discarded when their immediate use had passed. Perhaps the most beautiful objects here, which epitomise this attitude, are the two round fans, each made from a single palm leaf. I forget where they came from now - so many people used to, and I hope still do, make things like this. They are for fanning the embers of a fire and, had they not been given to me, they would have been thrown into the fire once singed. And yet they are exquisitely made, with a technique which has been handed down through the generations and may be thousands of years old. The material for making them is growing all around; there is no cost; they give aesthetic pleasure. We, who are surrounded by essential consumer goods, can barely imagine life where everyone can make everything that is needed, and will make it beautiful at the same time. These are the skills which made us human beings, homo sapiens, wise people, cleverer than our ancestors or animals, and the wisdom lay in the beauty.

Owen Jones (1809-1874), one of the most influential architects and designers of the 19th century (he decorated the Crystal Palace for the Great Exhibition), was probably the first person to recognise and admire the level of craftsmanship, style and ornamentation employed by what he called, in the language of his day 'savage tribes'. The leading authority on his work, Carol A. Hrvol Flores, writes: "Jones believed that the development of ornament preceded every other form of art and resulted from man's innate desire to produce forms of beauty evident in the works of nature. To prove his argument, he expanded the study of ornament to include the designs of "savages" (the Maori of New Zealand) [among others]. His recognition of the merit of their ornamental designs and his insistence that these were the result of instincts and aims common to all mankind was highly unusual in Victorian Britain where the people of the nonindustrial world were considered backward and uncivilized". Alas! A hundred and fifty years later such prejudices are still common.

I am neither an anthropologist nor an ethnographer and I make no pretence of understanding the cultural significance of these objects, nor the technology which went into their production. I am certain that the descriptions which follow will often be found wanting in the accuracy of their location, who made them and why. I only know that they were nearly all pressed on me, often during ceremonies or in the field, and that each one has for me a special memory, even though I may well have forgotten or transposed their exact origins over the years.

Having being given all these beautiful things and enjoyed having them, I want to give something back to those who made them. The best way I can do that is to sell them in aid of Survival International, so that the proceeds are used to support their descendants and help them to retain their land and their culture. Ideally, they will stay together, which is why we have put together this book.

Robin Hanbury-Tenison

DEDICATION TO NYPAUN

In 1977 I was invited by the Royal Geographical Society to lead what was to become the largest scientific expedition ever to leave these shores. For fifteen months we lived deep in the heart of Borneo in the newly created Gunung Mulu National Park looking after a hundred and twenty scientists from ten nations, who came and went, making the first full-scale, multidisciplinary study of a rainforest. It was from this research that the worldwide movement and campaign to protect rainforests grew. The scientists worked in remote sub camps, which we built in various terrains. A small team of us looked after them from the longhouse we built on traditional lines. There we had a doctor and nurse and local girls who washed their clothes in the river, as well as plenty of good food and drink.

One day early on, after we had been in Mulu for about two months and had only heard rumours that there might be nomads still in the forest, but had seen none, I was almost alone in Base Camp. I looked up and saw a figure standing motionless in the shade at the side of our clearing. He was naked except for a bark loincloth and he carried a blowpipe. For a frozen moment I still recall with a shiver our eyes met and then he walked over to me and took my hand. His name was Nyapun and I understood, as we sat and talked in our equally halting Malay, that his family were camped some way away to the north-east. The next morning early I trotted behind him for five hours and arrived in Paradise. His two wives and young children looked up like startled fawns as we approached their two sulaps or shelters. None of them, except Nyapun had seen a white man before. Reassured, they went back to what they were doing: the women to preparing wild sago by pounding and sieving it in bark containers; the children to searching for prawns and small fish in the stream below their camp. Later the eldest of his ten children, two sons, returned with a bearded pig (sus barbatus) slung on a pole between them. We feasted that night and they all returned with me to Base Camp, where they stayed for a year. Nyapun became my constant guide, companion and best friend. From then on I never had to worry about getting lost or running out of food when out on patrol and together we covered most of the Park and its surroundings.

Nyapun was a few years older than me and had led a remarkable life, as I was to find out one evening, when he told me his life story through a Berawan interpreter, who spoke both Penan and English fluently. "When I was a very young man, it was the time of the Japanese and Tuan Tom arrived here." [Tom Harrisson was the English officer who was parachuted into the Kelabit highlands in 1945 and mobilized the indigenous people against the Japanese forces then still occupying Borneo but starting to flee inland from the coast as the Allies attacked. He told the people that the prohibition against the traditional practice of headhunting had been lifted where the Japanese were concerned and very many were killed in this way.] "I had a very good time with Tuan Tom and we took many heads. Then he left and nothing much happened until Tuan Rodney arrived." [Rodney Needham, later to be Professor of Social Anthropology at Oxford, did his field work with the Penan in 1951/2]. "I travelled for many months with him, visiting my relations. About ten years later, my brother and I were hunting along the Melinau River when we saw a lot of white men in uniforms coming up the river in boats. We watched them setting up camp and then, without disturbing the sentries, we went into the tent of the head man and asked him what he was doing." [This was probably a visit made by the Royal Greenjackets in 1965 during Konfrontasi, the undeclared war between Britain and Indonesia, who opposed the creation of Malaysia. I would like to have seen the Colonel's face when Nyapun and his brother walked into his tent.] "Then we saw no more Europeans until you arrived."

When we eventually left, Nyapun and his family gathered on the river bank to see us off. One by one, his children came and forced bead bracelets they had made onto our wrists, or hung pretty necklaces around our necks. At last Nyapun and I embraced and the tears coursed unashamedly down both our faces. I knew how much he trusted me to help during the difficult years that inevitably lay ahead for him and his people; and I knew how little I would probably be able to do.

Nyapun is still alive as I write this in the summer of 2012. I have revisited him several times in the intervening years and hope to do so again. Because several of the artefacts here were given to me by him and because he taught me so much, I dedicate this book to him.

Robin Hanbury-Tenison

Nypaun at home, the day after we met.

Xingu Indian feather headdresses.

In 1971, when Marika and I stayed with the Villas Boas brothers in the Xingu National Park, there were about 1500 Indians from 15 tribes living there in harmony. Eleven Upper Xingu tribes were administered from Posto Leonardo and four from Diauarum, two day's journey by boat downstream. The Kamayura village was idyllically located beside a lagoon full of fish. The yellow headdress was presented to me after they danced the fish dance for us. The others are from different tribes, probably the Yawalapeti and the Juruna.

Xingu Indian combs and a monkey tooth necklace.

These exquisitely made pieces are just combs for daily use. The tight weaving in intricate traditional patterns is simply there for decoration and to help make them serviceable for a long time. But once broken or dirty, they will be thrown away. Few things last long in the rainforest. Monkeys used to be an important part of the diet and every part of the animal was used, including the teeth, which were made into treasured necklaces.

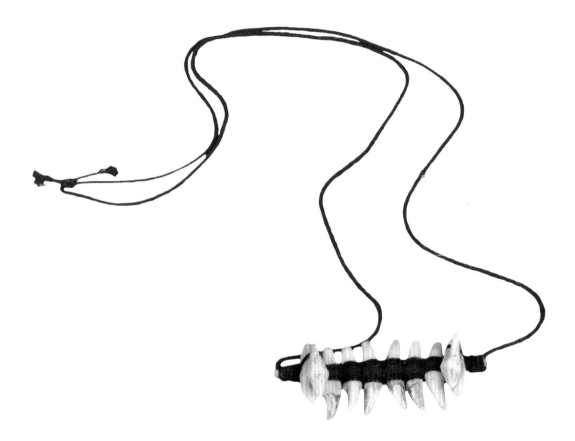

Amazonian Indian baskets and a calabash

We were given so many baskets by the Indians we visited that I cannot say which tribe made these. The patterns are traditional, the weaving tight and faultless. They were doubtless being used when we admired them. Before metal pots became available, calabashes were and still are the normal containers of food.

Waura pots.

The Waura are the only tribe among the Upper Xingu Indians who make pots traditionally. These were already being replaced with unbreakable metal pots, but many still preferred to use these for cooking. All were zoomorphic (representing animals) and this big one was a turtle. The small one is an armadillo.

Juruna pot and jaguar throne.

The Juruna were another tribe who made pots. They had moved into the lower part of the Xingu National Park fairly recently. This one they said represented a deer. When we visited them, the chief was sitting on this fine stool carved from a single piece of ironwood and representing a jaguar. He insisted I take it home with me when I made the mistake of admiring it.

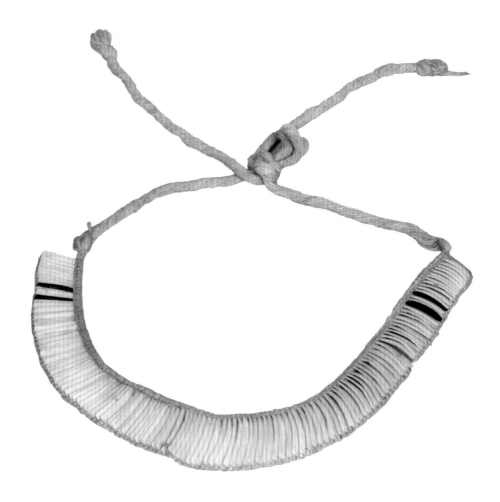

Kamayura Indian necklace.

Made from the shells of a large terrestrial snail, this ornament, called a mura pehi, is highly valued in the Upper Xingu and had taken five hundred hours to make. The carving is done with piranha teeth and the holes for stringing the pieces together are drilled with dogfish teeth. It was given to Marika by Claudio Villas Boas.

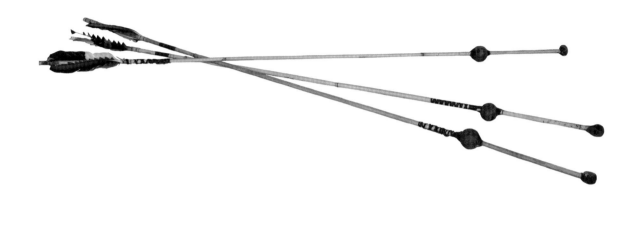

Suya arrows.

These extraordinary arrows were given to me by the Suya Indians in the Xingu National Park. The arrows had circular nuts attached part way up the shaft with a hole cut in them, which caused the arrow to whistle when it was fired into the air. The feather fletches were curved like a propeller, thus making an even more interesting noise. The purpose was to hypnotise the target bird into remaining on its perch high in a tree instead of flying away, as it might do had it heard the usual swish of an arrow. The arrows, instead of having killing points, simply had a lump of beeswax on the end designed to stun the bird and make it fall to the ground, when it would be taken home to be kept as a pet for its tail feathers. They demonstrated the technique for us, firing arrows high in the air so that they made their strange fluty whistle before turning at the top of their arc and plummeting to earth, scattering the crowd of watching children.

Txukarramai club.

These clubs, called kukanga, are used to hunt wild boar and other animals by running them down and striking them, instead of using bows and arrows. This one had been used in battles against the then still uncontacted Kreen Akrore tribe, we were told. Formidably well balanced, it is made of iron-hard wood. Similar clubs were used to kill Richard Mason, when he was ambushed by the Kreen Akrore ten years before I was given this one by Claudio Villas Boas in 1971. Some were left beside his body. I had been offered one of these in Buenos Aires in 1965 by Eduardo Barros Prado, an old Brazilian explorer, who had been a guide on a Hamilton Rice Amazon expedition in the 1920s. He had been a member of the party which went in to bring Richard's body out.

Yanomami Arrows.

The Yanomami make arrows up to seven feet long from bamboo and cane. Preparing them takes up more of a man's time than any other activity.   Matching sections of plumes from parrots, macaws and black curassow are set on opposite sides of the shaft and bound into place with lengths of cotton. Barbs are made of monkey bone for birds and sharpened palm wood for monkeys, bound with fibre and held fast with resin.

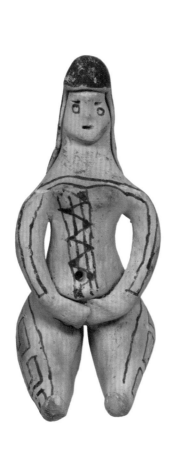

Karaja Pottery

I first visited the Karaja Indians on the island of Bananal in 1958 with Richard Mason; and then again in 1971 with Marika. They are famous for making ceramic figures as dolls for their children. These often have the heavy thighs familiar from much pre-Columbian art, representing fertility and feminine beauty. Pottery is the exclusive preserve of the women, who also make models of animals and birds, as well as pots for domestic use.

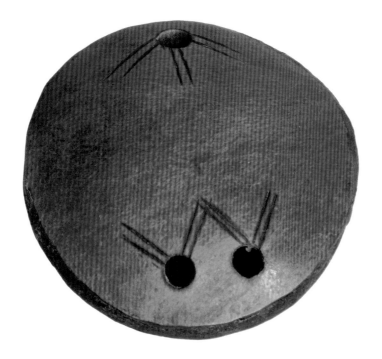

Nambiquara nose flute

These very unusual flutes, unique to the Nambiquara, are made from two slightly curved sides of a large golden seed, stuck together with beeswax and decorated with a pattern burnt into the wood. There are three holes: one for blowing through, using one nostril, the other two for fingers to stop and so vary the notes. When we were staying with the tribe, one man would start playing, filling the hut with haunting, birdlike calls. Soon answering notes would be heard from another hut and together they would play a warbling, complicated, magical tune.

Yanomami hammock and a universal tool.

In 1981 I lived for a time with the Yanomami preparing an illustrated book for Time Life (sadly now out of print). Their large communal buildings are called yanos. Bruce Albert, the French anthropologist, Victor Englebert, the Belgian photographer and I (the writer) slept in the Toototobi yano in cotton Brazilian hammocks. Our hosts preferred ones made from strips of bark, like this one, claiming they were more comfortable. Many Yanomami men in our yano carried a small tool on a string round the neck. This was made from an agouti tooth and served many purposes, being sharp and very hard it could cut through anything.

Tuareg sandal (ératim)

From Agadez, Niger, these are the original flip flops. They are ideal for the Tuareg, as they can be put on quickly by camel riders, who ride barefoot, but need to be able to protect their feet when dismounting onto hot sand and acacia thorns. Made from two layers of untanned ox-hide, which have been beaten on stone, softened in wet sand, greased with butter and then covered with a tanned piece of dyed and decorated sheepskin, they are considered the most beautiful footwear.

Tuareg amulet and stone carvings.

All the Tuareg I travelled with had one or more leather amulets or gri-gri around their necks. These contained charms to protect them on their long journeys. I was given this unusual metal one by an old man in Djanet, the oasis in the Tassili n'Ajjer Mountains in Algeria, from which I set off on my first camel journey in search of prehistoric rock art in 1961. He assured me that it was especially efficacious as protection against snake bite and sword thrust. I have worn it on all my subsequent camel journeys and it has never let me down!

The carvings, of a tortoise, a dagger and a cup, are made from a hard local stone. These came from a nomadic family I met deep in the Aïr Mountains, when I was travelling by camel in 2003. It was so unlikely to find them being offered for sale where no tourists ever went that I bought them.

Toubou and Tuareg daggers.

Toubou women in the Tibesti Mountains of Northern Chad, where I travelled with John Hemming in 1965, were very independent. They made long caravan journeys without men and usually carried daggers, which were larger and much more tasselled than those worn by the men. Those were small and lethal, worn strapped to the arm and concealed below the robe. The Tuareg also carried small daggers (télek), as well as the long swords (takuba). This unusual brass dagger was given to me in Iferouane in 1966 by Arambé, the Tuareg with whom I first travelled for three weeks into the Aïr Mountains in search of prehistoric rock art.

Tuareg calabash butter container.

Goats' milk is churned in an inflated camel hide bag and then stored in a calabash.
Soft, white cheese, which is quite delicious, is also made using similar utensils.

Tuareg saddlebags.

Called in Tamachek, the Tuareg language, ejjebira, these huge saddle bags used only to be made in Agadez. The tanned leather is richly decorated with fringes and hanging tassels, and with geometric designs in many different colours. The fine patterns are daubed on with a small knife and each hole is punched with an awl. They were all I took with me as baggage on my camels.

A Fulani hat.

The cattle herding Fulani or Peul's territory overlaps with that of the Tuareg and I acquired this hat in Agadez. These particular hats are worn by men to attract women, as well as being very comfortable. Cowrie shells, which used to be common currency in the Sahara, are sometimes used as decoration.

A replica Tuareg camel saddle.

I wanted to bring one of my saddles home with me, but it was just too heavy and would have caused all sorts of problems with customs. Also the cruciform pommel is very fragile. One of the problems riding a proper Tuareg saddle is resisting the temptation to cling on to the pommel in order to avoid falling off. This is strictly forbidden!

Straw jewellery from Timbuktu.

When passing theough Timbuktu in 1966, I found someone selling this remarkably realistic
'gold jewellery'. They told that it was a craft which had developed because they had seen gold
objects being carried on the slave caravans which passed through their town over the centuries
and,being too poor ever to afford gold, they had made their own replicas out of straw.

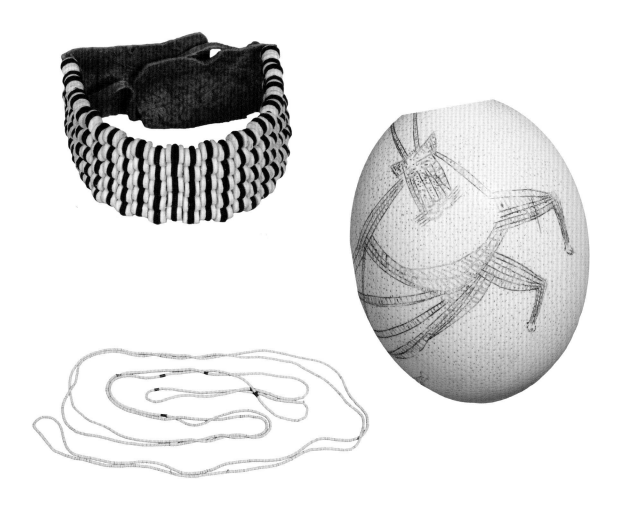

Kalahari ostrich egg bracelet, necklace and decorated egg.

In 1980 I walked across part of the Kalahari desert with a Bushman called Ebenene. He threw away my water bottle and gave me this egg, which he had decorated with a gemsbok. He filled it each day from sip wells, sucking the water up into his mouth with a straw and dribbling it into the egg. One fill was my daily ration. His wife gave me the necklace, which is made from little rings painstakingly shaped from bits of ostrich egg. The bracelet I bought.

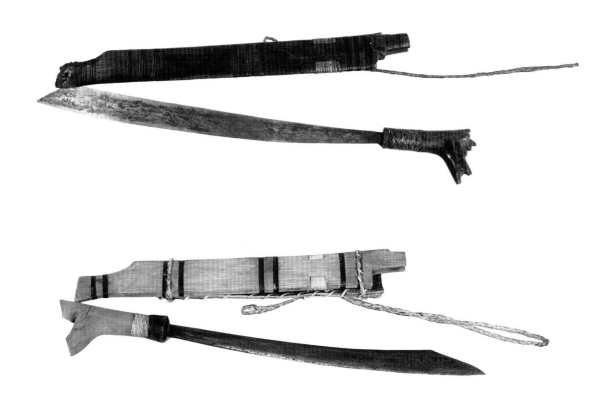

Ancient and modern Borneo parangs.

I was presented with this ancient parang at a ceremony in the Berawan longhouse, from which I had recruited most of the labour force for the Royal Geographical Society expedition to Mulu in Sarawak. They told me that the blade, which was very old, had taken a hundred heads. The scabbard they had made recently. They gave me the tribal name Oyau Abeng, which means Prince of the Mountain, a legendary folk hero, who was immortal and able to grow a new limb if one was cut off. My deputy, Nigel Winser, they named Tebenggang, who was Oyau Abeng's loyal squire.

The other parang is a normal modern implement, as carried by everyone travelling in the forest. It is needed all the time for everything from cutting a path to removing leeches. This is the one I used most of the time I was on the Mulu expedition.

Penan blowpipe and quivers.

Nyapun gave me this blowpipe and the quiver containing poisoned darts. There is also a clever little tool for shaping the wads of fibre, which go on the ends of the darts, so that they fit exactly and fly true. Drilling the hole through the very hard wood of the blowpipe is a most laborious business, which takes many weeks. The poison for the darts is said to have no antidote and it is much stronger than the curare used in South America. It is extracted from the bark of the upas tree (Antiaris toxicaria). The quiver on the left is from another trip.

Bark loincloth.

A bark loincloth, or cawat, given to me by Nyapun. It is similar to the one he was wearing when we first met.
Everyone agreed that these were much more comfortable than cloth ones. Once they were the standard
dress of the Iban and of all the Dayak people of Borneo, to be replaced in the nineteenth and twentieth
centuries by colourful ones made from cloth, but few people wear even those much any more today. This
one is made from a long strip of inner bark from the ipoh tree, which is favoured because of its softness.
Beating it for a long time with a grooved wooden mallet makes it even softer and gives it texture.

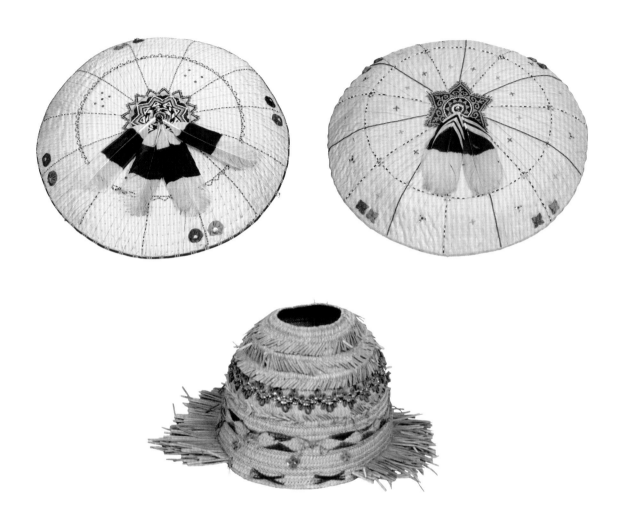

Berawan hats.

These large hats from the Baram River, Sarawak, are as functional as they are decorative. When spending all day in a narrow dugout on the river, alternately scorched by the tropical sun and deluged by torrential rain, they are a lifesaver. Made from nipah palm leaves, the adornments are coloured shells and beads in time-honoured patterns. The hornbill feathers denote, we were told, that the owner had taken a head. Headhunting was abolished by the Rajahs Brooke in the early twentieth century, and only briefly resuscitated in the battle to remove the Japanese at the end of World War II. It seems therefore unlikely that these hats, albeit quite old, had been owned by one who had taken heads in his youth.

This small decorated Berawan hat was only worn by a man on special occasions in the longhouse, when much borak (fermented rice wine) would be drunk and everyone, hosts and visitors alike, would be expected to dance

Penan baskets.

These are the iconic craft of the Penan and they are today one of their main sources of income from sales to tourists. Beautifully made from rattan, with the finest of basket weaving, a good one is practically waterproof when travelling through the rainforest.

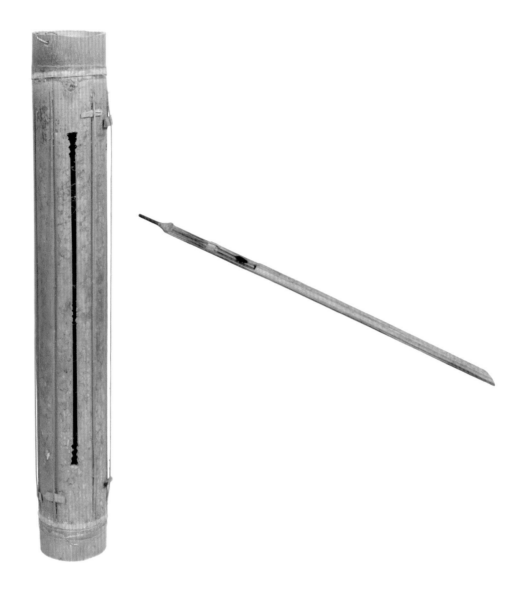

Penan musical instruments.

Perhaps the oldest stringed instrument in the world is the pagang. It is made from a big piece of hollow bamboo, on which strips have been raised to create strings. They produce a mellow twang when plucked. The oreng is a type of jew's harp made from a thin sliver of sago palm wood. It makes lovely sad notes, which can be very beguiling. The Penan, like the Nambiquara, have nose flutes, but these look more like normal flutes.

Penan bead necklaces and bracelets.

As anyone who travelled with the Penan in the old days knows, these laboriously made decorations were forced over a visitor's head or hands on arrival and departure. By the same token, beads were one of the most acceptable presents. Today these artefacts form an important part of the income of settled Penan, when the opportunity arises to sell them to passing tourists.

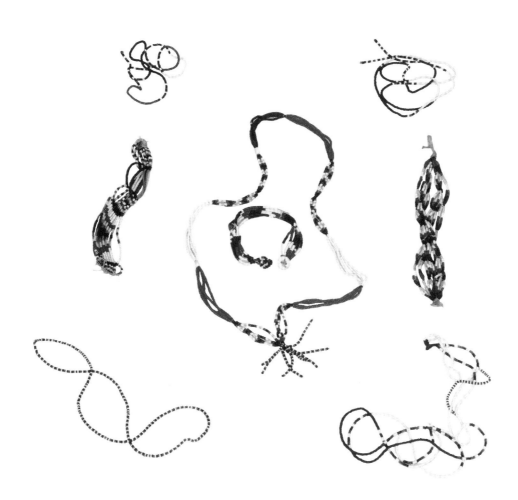

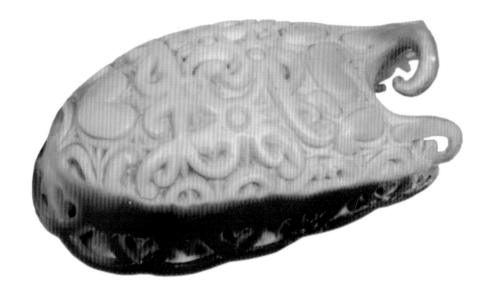

Rhinoceros Hornbill earring.

A rare carved earring made from the casque of a rhinoceros hornbill, which is the national bird of Sarawak. This material and that taken from its relation, the helmeted hornbill, was traded for centuries from Borneo to China, where its value was greater than gold. Today, the birds are protected as an endangered species and the trade is strictly prohibited.

Kelabit salt cellars.

The Kelabit of Borneo's central highlands make their own salt by boiling the saline water from special springs. Once all the water is gone, the salt is dried and put in decorated bamboo tubes. It is highly prized. I visited the springs and still have some of the salt I acquired then, which I regularly use and maintain it keeps me young.

Borneo fishing charms

I acquired these bone figurines many years ago in Borneo, probably in Miri. I was told that they are charms, which are sunk with the bait and attract the fish. I can find out nothing more about them. Perhaps someone will enlighten me.

A Dani stone digging tool.

The existence of the Dani people living in the Baliem Valley in the centre of the Indonesian part of the island of new Guinea only became known to the outside world in 1938, when spotted from the air. In 1973 they were beginning to trade for metal tools with the outside world but most work in their rectangular and fertile sweet potato gardens was still being done with implements made from stone. Inside one of their dark, low houses we saw neat stacks of bows and arrows and flint-stoned axes with their finely polished heads attached to handles hewn from hardwood at an angle, strapped on by lengths of narrow vine. These were used for cutting down trees as well as clearing the ground and hoeing. The blue-grey stones, as hard as metal, and finely honed to a sharp edge, came from a secret place outside the valley and were valued by the Dani ritually as well as for their function.

Asmat nose bones.

All the Asmat men we met on the south coast of Indonesian New Guinea had perforated septums through which they inserted bones. Usually these were made from the leg bone of a pig, but we were told that one of these three was a human bone. I forget which.

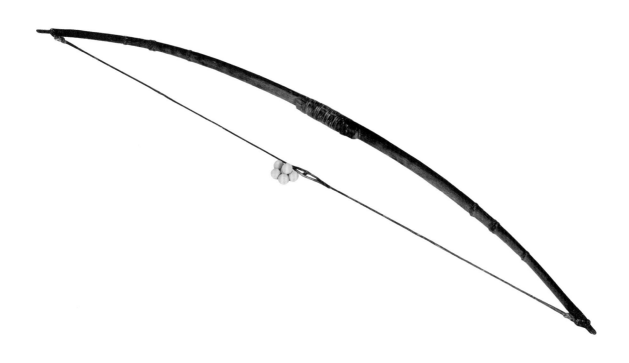

Kurmi 'marble' bow from Arunachalam Pradesh, N.E. India.

I was given this most unusual bow, from which clay balls or marbles are fired, by a man who described himself as a Kurmi tribal from the State of Bihar. We were in a very remote corner of North East India: Tirap Province in the State of Arunachal Pradesh, which lies on the borders of Nagaland and Burma (Myanmar). His name was Bhubon Kurmi and he said the bow was called a gooti dhenzu. He demonstrated how it should be used, holding it upright like a normal bow and arrow, but with the string out to the side.

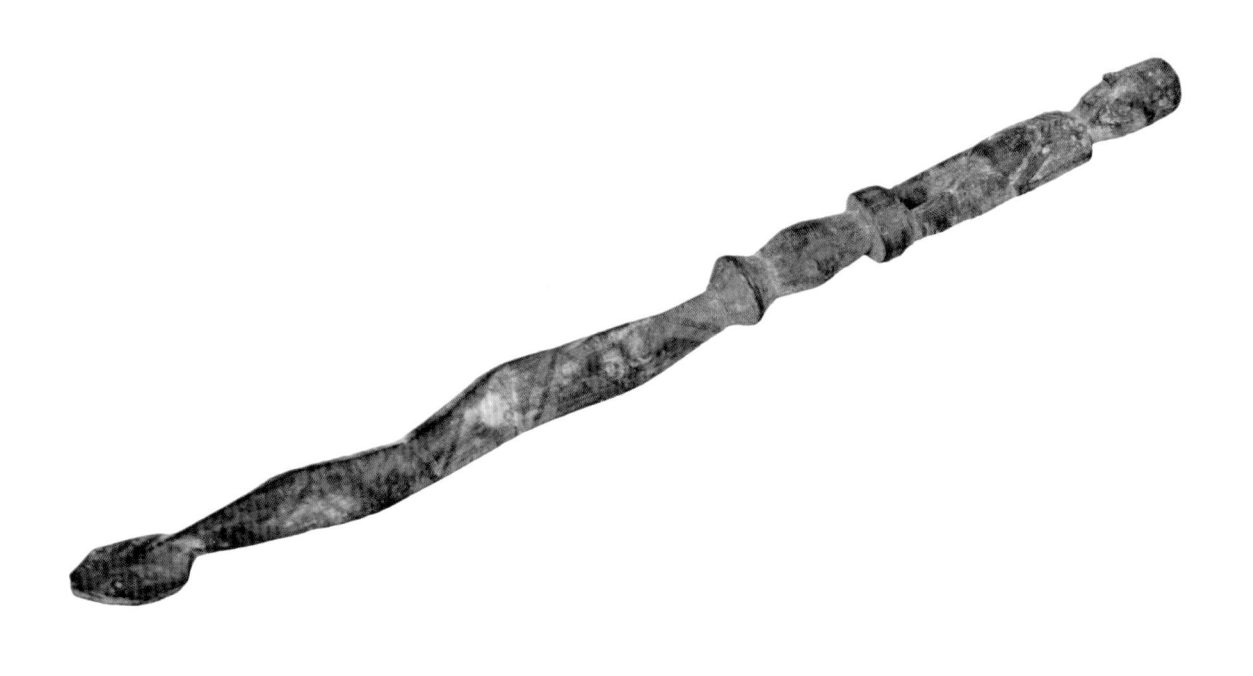

Embera Choco ceremonial wand.

When I set off in 1972 to travel with the Embera Choco Indians in Panama to cross the watershed to the Pacific coast, their chief gave me this ceremonial wand, which he said had great power, to protect me. It did.

Fans from I forget where.

I regard these as among the most beautiful artefacts I possess, and yet they are intrinsically valueless. I have seen similar fans being used by tribal people all over the world to keep fires alight and forget where these came from, but that doesn't really matter. What they tell us is that many of the technically poorest people make some of the most elegant things, and do so purely for their own satisfaction.

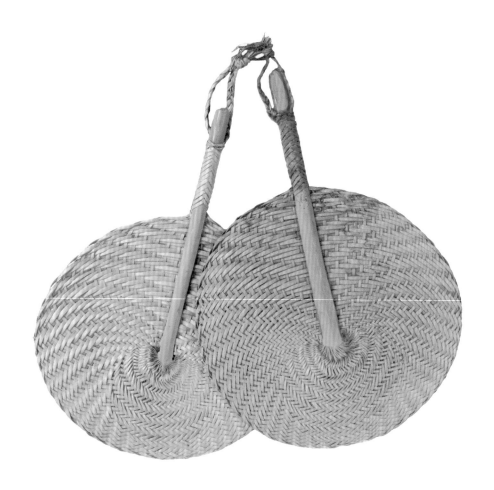